Close! that Sale

The Mini-Bible for Every Sales Guy!

by Mark Jenkins

Copyright © 2018 Mark Jenkins

All Rights Reserved

Preface

Close that Sale! Why? Because You need to, because they need as well. On one hand it boosts your business and on the other it satisfies the needs of the buyer. Think about it as a way ...a doctor cures the patient; an engineer repairs the machine and an architect builds your house; so is The Salesman who serves the needs of the buyer!

You don't believe it? Don't blame yourself. Around the world because of shortages and a controlled economy, we haven't had much experience of competition, where our businessmen have to really put in an effort to sell. But times are changing fast. Now business success depends more and more on a really professional sales effort.

The difference between a professional and a non-professional is that a professional think of his professionalism first. The criterion for professionalism in selling is the ability to think rationally of your prospect - his needs, expectations and capabilities. Like a doctor or an engineer, a professional salesperson uses a variety of skills which are detailed for you in this book.

But before we get there, we need to remove some misconceptions about salespeople. First, *salesman* is almost a dirty word. Most people think of salesmen as using all techniques, including dishonesty, deception and other underhanded methods to get the order. He may be totally misinformed and have no intension to fulfil the needs of his prospect; his only concern is to get his pay or his commission. In fact, this is a good portrait of the *High-Pressure Salesman-* but the Professional Salesman is quite different.

The professional thinks of his prospect first, last and always, knowing the commissions will flow in automatically. Doctors, engineers, chartered accountants do the same, don't they? A doctor thinks of curing his patient first, and therefore society respects doctors.

In many countries successful salespeople enjoy a good reputation and respect in society. Such salespeople may not go through college as doctors do. They learn their profession by observing other successful salespeople and by attending courses. They learn from competitors as well. In the final analysis, the customer, being the boss, decides a salesperson's success. The professional salesperson knows that his best customers are the geese that can lay golden eggs, and he respects and nurtures them with sincerity.

Another misconception about salespeople is the idea that they are sup-posed to talk and talk and talk. No! A good salesperson listens to his prospect carefully, asks several short questions, and does not interrupt. This way, he finds out how he can give the most suitable product to the prospect at the least cost. THINK! Put yourself in the shoes of a customer for a moment, and think back which salesperson you respect; obviously the one who helped you fulfil your needs most efficiently.

Perhaps the most critical thing that the professional salesperson needs to understand is this: successful selling has three components, namely product knowledge, selling skills and selling attitude, but their ranking in importance is surprising.

Product knowledge - 10%

Selling skills - 20%

Selling attitude - 70%

As in most things you do in life, your attitude makes the difference!

This little book is meant as a kind of checklist, to help you keep your selling skills and attitude in top form. If you consult it regularly your salesmanship is sure to be both professional and successful.

Table of Contents

The Six Steps of Selling

The Five Facts about You and Your Customers

    THE CUSTOMER IS THE BOSS.

    THE CUSTOMER IS THE PROFIT; EVERYTHING ELSE IS OVERHEAD.

    YOU MUST PUT YOURSELF IN YOUR CUSTOMER'S SHOES.

    WHY CUSTOMERS QUIT

    YOU ARE NOT JUST MAKING SALES; YOU ARE CREATING CUSTOMERS.

Four Cues to Better Communication

    FOCUS ON WHAT YOU NEED TO FIND OUT.

    MAINTAIN TWO-WAY COMMUNICATION AT ALL TIMES.

    WATCH YOUR THREE A'S: APPEARANCE, ATTITUDE AND APPROACH.

    MIND YOUR LANGUAGE.

Six Practical Pointers for Showroom Selling

    GIVE A FRIENDLY AND ENTHUSIASTIC GREETING.

    SELL YOURSELF.

    CREATE CONFIDENCE ABOUT YOUR ORGANISATION.

    QUALIFY THE CUSTOMER.

    DEMONSTRATE YOUR EQUIPMENT.

    ANSWER HIS QUESTIONS.

Three Tips for Sales Prospecting through Mail Shots and Letters

- YOU DO NEED REGULAR PROSPECTING.
- DIRECT MAIL CAN BE AN EXTREMELY EFFECTIVE WEAPON IN YOUR
- PUT "MARKETING MAGIC" INTO YOUR DIRECT MAIL.

Six Better Ways to Outsell Your Competitors

- NEVER SPEAK ILL OF YOUR COMPETITORS.
- KNOW YOUR COMPETITORS.
- KNOW YOUR COMPETITORS' PRODUCTS AND ACTIVITIES AS WELL AS
- LOSE ONE, GAIN TWO.
- CALL ON YOUR COMPETITORS' CUSTOMERS REGULARLY.
- SHADOW THE SALESPEOPLE OF YOUR COMPETITORS.

Seven Stories for Salespeople

- IF I DON'T GO, I DON'T GET.
- ASK YOUR CUSTOMERS…
- JUDGE BY SALES, NOT BY REPORTS.
- WHERE YOU HEAR A DOOR CLOSE, I HEAR IT OPEN…
- THE WAR WAS LOST BECAUSE OF A NAIL.
- BE CLEAR ABOUT YOUR MARKET SEGMENT.
- SALESMEN ARE NOT ORDER-TAKERS.

Nine Sales Objections and How to Handle Them

- I CAN'T AFFORD IT.

I AM NOT INTERESTED.

I WILL THINK IT OVER.

COME BACK IN THIRTY DAYS.

JUST LEAVE ME YOUR LITERATURE.

I AM HAPPY WITH MY PRESENT DEALER.

MY JOB IS DIFFERENT.

I'LL HAVE TO TALK IT OVER WITH MY FATHER.

I WILL WAIT UNTIL BUSINESS IS BETTER.

The Secret of Selling Well

The Six Steps of Selling

In every sale there are six steps which a prospect and you have to take together.

Attention. You have to get the prospect's attention, either at his doorstep or by attracting him to your showroom, so that you can draw him into conversation to find out his needs.

Interest. You have to arouse his curiosity so he becomes hungry to know more about your product. Testimonials can be an excellent way, especially in India where many prospects are first-time buyers.

Conviction. Now you have to convince your prospect that your product will meet his needs. To do so, you have to have confidence in yourself, your dealership and the product, and, you have to show enthusiasm for what you are selling, and that comes from your motivation and positive attitude.

Desire. You have to arouse the desire in your prospect's mind, convincing him that your product will meet his needs easily and that he will get a bit more as bonus too.

Close. Close the sale or you will be just wasting your time and working for your competitors. Work systematically and ask for the order if the prospect has given you signals, he is ready to buy. Otherwise, go back and ask more questions so you can fill in the missing links.

Congratulate. When your prospect has said yes, congratulate him. His decision means money to you, and he needs reassurance that his decision is correct. Once he gives his money you must proceed to thank him. Please note the difference between congratulating and thanking.

The Five Facts about You and Your Customers

THE CUSTOMER IS THE BOSS.

There never has been, there is not now, and there never will be any boss but the customer.

He is the one boss you must please.

Everything you own he has paid for.

He buys your home, cars and clothes.

He pays for your vacations and puts your children through school.

He pays your doctor's bills and writes every pay check you will ever receive.

He will give you every promotion you will ever obtain during your lifetime.

And he will discharge you if you displease him.

THE CUSTOMER IS THE PROFIT; EVERYTHING ELSE IS OVERHEAD.

The customer is the only goose that lays golden eggs every day forever. So, we must care for him.

Over service present customers a little bit because they are and will continue to be your best prospects for more business.

Use your mind's eye to remove the small difficulties and anxieties of your customers.

If a business is sailing with a heavy load of overhead, it will gradually sink to the bottom of the market ocean. Eliminate all those activities which are not related to helping your customers.

YOU MUST PUT YOURSELF IN YOUR CUSTOMER'S SHOES.

The one who wears the shoes is the one who knows where the shoes pinch. Right? To understand what hurts as well as heartens customers, you have to put yourself in their shoes.

Make sure you do not ignore or cheat the customer, and pay full attention to what he says.

Spend ten minutes every day thinking how you can put yourself into your customers' shoes. Listen to your customers; ask them questions; look into their eyes.

Start thinking good of your customers, and start doing good to your customers in your working as well as sleeping hours.

WHY CUSTOMERS QUIT

1%   die

3%   move away

5%   form other friendships

9%   for competitive reasons

14% because of product dissatisfaction

68% because of attitude of indifference on the part of an employee.

WHY CUSTOMERS QUIT?

A brief explanation..

As salespeople, we do not have much control over the first 9% who die, move away or form other friendships.

As for the 9% who move to competitors, we should not curse the competition. We should be thankful for competition because it's what keeps us on our toes. We should also be pulling away 9% from them to keep the balance.

As for the next 14%, we must remember that our product is a package of what we sell and the after-sales service. If either is inadequate or inferior it's up to us to improve it.

The last 68%-the major chunk-is completely within our control. Remember, the customer is spending his hard-earned money to buy our product. If we are inconsiderate or indifferent to him he has every right to take his money to where he is attended to properly.

YOU ARE NOT JUST MAKING SALES; YOU ARE CREATING CUSTOMERS.

No customers, no business. It's just as simple as that, but so easy to forget as well.

Meet your customers personally. Don't hide inside your air-conditioned office, look for opportunities to meet your customers-you can never overdo it.

Become trustworthy to your customers. Lose your profits, if you have to, but honour your promises and commitments. Even the most ordinary looking customer is a decision-maker in his own house, and he has enough common sense to see through your intentions to your trustworthiness. When you think you can outsmart him, you are only fooling yourself in the long run.

Deeds count more than words. One small deed for your customer accomplishes more than a thousand words.

Four Cues to Better Communication

Keep your eye on the ball.

FOCUS ON WHAT YOU NEED TO FIND OUT.

What are the real needs of the prospect? What does he want? There may be a difference. A prospect may want a certain product because it looks good, or because it's the latest model, or his friend has one, even though it may not solve his problems. A professional salesman sells what his prospect needs.

Can the prospect take the decision to buy, or does he have to check with his father, boss...? You need to know who the real influencers and decision-makers are.

Does the prospect have money now, or will he need financial assistance?

What is the Dominant Buying Motive (DBM)? Is it a marriage gift? Is it to show off? Is it to solve a practical problem? Is it an impulse, or something he's been thinking about for a long time? The sale depends more than 50% on knowing this.

MAINTAIN TWO-WAY COMMUNICATION AT ALL TIMES.

Determine his main interest. You can do it by asking him a few questions. Observe how he is dressed. Listen to what he says; let it go into your head and keep it for possible use later.

Gain and keep understanding. Use words which he understands. Talk slowly and clearly. Do not be too technical (please reject the temptation to show off your knowledge). Frequently, but humbly, ask if he understands and, if need be, repeat what you have said, slowly.

Listen, listen, listen... Salesmen normally do not listen. They think they have to talk and talk, whether or not the prospect is listening. This is WRONG. A salesman should be as professional as a doctor or a chartered accountant. Don't they listen and then talk? In between, they ask questions to get more information.

WATCH YOUR THREE A'S: APPEARANCE, ATTITUDE AND APPROACH.

Your appearance says a lot to your prospect. Make sure it's neat and smart, neither overdone nor sloppy.

Remember that your attitude always shows. Keep it positive.

If your approach conveys the desire to be helpful you will set the ground to proceed.

Remember!

> "A smile is the universal language understood around the world…"

MIND YOUR LANGUAGE.

The most important factor in deciding whether the prospect will become your customer is the first impression that he receives.

The way you stand or sit, the way you allow your hands or feet to behave, the way your facial muscles are arranged and of course the words you use will create the first impression.

Greet the customer promptly. With a smile in your voice ask him what you can do for him today.

Listen without interrupting.

Don't react. Listen, think, then speak.

Never say "I can't help you."

Provide complete information.

Don't make promises you cannot keep.

Remember, the customer must be made to believe that he is welcome and that he is valued, always.

Six Practical Pointers for Showroom Selling

BUSINESS GOES

WHERE IT IS INVITED

AND STAYS

WHERE IT IS WELL TREATED.

GIVE A FRIENDLY AND ENTHUSIASTIC GREETING.

Meet the customer at the door or even before he gets inside the showroom.

Use the customer's name if you know it.

This makes a favourable first impression and also provides you with an opportunity to analyse the customer.

Remember, many a sale has been won or lost in the first 90 seconds.

THINK POSITIVE… BECOME POSITIVE.

Change your thoughts, and you change your world.

SELL YOURSELF.

And questions that involve the customer and get across the idea that you are interested in him.

Be a good listener.

Look for clues that point to his possible needs.

Think of the customer as an onion…use more questions to peel off the layers. Probe deeply for his needs, but be careful not to gouge and gash; the customer must not feel hurt or offended.

Your interest in the customer and enthusiasm for your work will strike a positive chord.

CREATE CONFIDENCE ABOUT YOUR ORGANISATION.

Convey to the customer that you represent a good company.

Let him know that the products you want to sell to him are backed up by the manufacturer and by you as the salesperson in your area.

If you are selling consumer durables, let him know about your Spare Parts Department and your Service Department.

Display your trophies, or other proof that you represent a reputable company.

Proudly show the customer your list of satisfied customers. You simply have to say, "Ask them."

ANY CUSTOMER WALKING INTO YOUR SHOWROOM IS LIKE THE PROVERBIAL GOOSE. EXTRACT ONE EGG PER VISIT AND GO IN FOR REPEAT BUSINESS. DON'T TRY TO MAKE A FAST BUCK AND VANISH OVERNIGHT.

YOU SHOULD BE IN BUSINESS FOR ATLEAST SIX GENERATIONS.

QUALIFY THE CUSTOMER.

Lead the customer into talking about his needs

Get him to acknowledge that he has a need.

Get a commitment that he will buy today if he gets the right deal.

"PUSSY CATS DON'T CLOSE SALES..."

"...BUT TIGERS CLOSE SALES AND MAKE FRIENDS TOO"

Become A Tiger Salesman!

DEMONSTRATE YOUR EQUIPMENT.

Every good car salesman does it. Guide the customer into the driver's seat; he will feel comfortable and proud; soon he will be thinking of his old car as junk...

It works with any product. Let the customer get to feel the importance of ownership of the product.

Of course, be careful. A countess should not be put into the driver's seat and told about automatic gear shifts; she should be guided into the rear seat and told about the soft leather upholstery.

Agreements get better results than arguments.

ANSWER HIS QUESTIONS.

Find out the customer's needs

Answer the customer's questions one by one.

Do not answer questions that he has not asked- unless the answers are positive in relation to your competition.

Do not argue with the customer; agreeing gets more sales.

Where possible, talk with the customer in a setting where disturbances and distractions are least, where you can talk to him comfortably, give him the relevant information and build confidence about yourself and your organisation.

Three Tips for Sales Prospecting through Mail Shots and Letters

Always remember that people don't plan to fail, they just fail to plan.

YOU DO NEED REGULAR PROSPECTING.

Without adequate prospecting, you will never even see many of the people who could be your customers.

Professional prospecting means using every method at your command to uncover a steady flow of good prospects.

You need regular prospecting because:

+ The prospect will forget you

+ The competition might sell to him

+ You want to get referrals

+ You need new customers

+ You need to monitor the changes in customers' needs

In every industry or product area there is a "rule of thumb" relationship between potential customers contracted and actual sales per month-in the tractor business, for example, it's 300 to 30. find out the figures for your business.

THE PEN IS MIGHTIER THAN THE SWORD

DIRECT MAIL CAN BE AN EXTREMELY EFFECTIVE WEAPON IN YOUR TOTAL SELLING ARMOURY.

Research shows that most people read it, provided the material is attractive and well presented.

Mailings can be coordinated to compliment or follow-up advertisements.

Mailings are an excellent way to establish contact with customers in advance of visits by sales staff.

You can pin-point your readership target, i.e. your most likely customers, very accurately.

A direct mail promotion is simple to organise, and you have plenty of options.

Business is like riding a bicycle-either you keep moving or you fall down.

PUT "MARKETING MAGIC" INTO YOUR DIRECT MAIL.

Make sure you have the three essential ingredients of your mail shot: letter, order form and reply envelope.

Write a "talking letter" –personal, to the point, no jargon.

Sell one thing at a time. More confuses the buyer and reduces the response.

Don't sell the product, sell the benefits, i.e. what the product will do for the customer.

Offer a long-term money-back guarantee.

Use P.S. to tell your reader what to do or think- surveys show that four out of five read the P.S. first and then keep it in mind as they read the letter.

Six Better Ways to Outsell Your Competitors

ALWAYS SMILE...

NEVER SPEAK ILL OF YOUR COMPETITORS.

Follow the "Holi" principle: if you sprinkle scented water on your friends they will do that to you, and if you darken their faces, they will do the same to you even better!

More important, your customers will not believe you when you run down your competitors and their products.

The best way to beat your competitors is to serve your customers better. Tell all about your products-what they can and cannot do to fulfil the needs of your prospect. And then shut up!

If your prospect asks for comparisons, do so only with testimonials, published data, well established facts.

When visiting your competitors, do not challenge their beliefs since you can't change them in a first meeting.

Follow the **SWOT** principle:

Concentrate on your **STRENGTHS**

Recognise your **WEAKNESSES**

Evaluate your **OPPORTUNITIES**

Research your **THREATS**

KNOW YOUR COMPETITORS.

You run your business for profit and for fun too. So, get rid of the common belief that your competitors are you enemies. No, sir, they are your friends. Life is too short to have enemies!

Befriend the competitors in your area, and call on them. Keep an updated SWOT analysis of each of your competitors. We all have strengths and weaknesses: you need to sell your strengths against your competitors' weaknesses.

When visiting your competitor give him your sincere compliments. Accept his good techniques, facilities, and so on. There are very good chances that he will reciprocate. And do tell him about yourself.

If your competitor visits your office, respect him. In several cases, we have seen local businessmen forming an association and this can give benefit for all.

COURAGE FACES FEAR AND THEREBY MASTERS IT. COWARDICE REPRESSES FEAR AND IS THEREBY MASTERED BY IT.

-Martin Luther King

KNOW YOUR COMPETITORS' PRODUCTS AND ACTIVITIES AS WELL AS YOUR OWN.

Remember, when a prospect comes to you, he has already visited your competitors or is likely to do so later, so you cannot hide the strengths of the competitors' products.

A prospect will respect you if you know your competitors' products well. You will lose him if you try to lie or bluff.

Once you have the SWOT analysis of each make and model of the products you sell, you will be able to talk to your prospects with confidence and conviction.

Keep in mind that as brand parties become a reality (competitive products are alike because each catch up with the others very fast or disappears altogether), the "product" is no longer just the widget. It is a package consisting of the product along with service support, training support, technical input, etc.

Adversity introduces a man to himself.

LOSE ONE, GAIN TWO.

You are also going to lose some sales. What do you do then? Do you hit the bottle, blame your dealership, blame your company, blame your luck? Or, do you consider it part of the game and get busy analysing to find out what's wrong?

You can learn big, real big lessons from such defeats. It is very important that you analyse every sale you make as well as every sale you lose. This is the way to build confidence and capability.

It is essential to relax and think after a lost sale. Find out what went wrong, regroup your energies and fine-tune your approach. Do not call or meet the next prospect unless you have re-conditioned yourself to be in top form to make the sale.

In this way the successful salesperson can be sure that if he loses one customer, he moves on to gain two.

STARVE THE PROBLEMS FEED THE OPPORTUNITIES

CALL ON YOUR COMPETITORS' CUSTOMERS REGULARLY.

Your competitors' customers can tell you a lot about your competitors' strengths and weaknesses, as they see them from the customers' point of view.

Your competitors' customers can tell you the plus and minus points of the competitor's product, since he has bought it and used it for some time.

A new customer of your competitor can reveal to you why he did not buy your product-you will come to know your weaknesses and this will help you to remove them.

If you meet such a customer frequently you also develop a rapport with him which can help break the ice toward winning him to your product when he goes for a repeat purchase or when his friends buy a similar product.

THE ULTIMATE MEASURE OF A MAN IS NOT WHERE HE STANDS IN MOMENTS

OF COMFORT AND CONVENIENCE, BUT WHERE HE STANDS AT TIMES OF CHALLENGE AND CONTROVERSY.

-Martin Luther King

SHADOW THE SALESPEOPLE OF YOUR COMPETITORS.

Observe your competitors, for they are the first ones to discover your faults.

Make monitoring of your competitors' part of your programme. It is an activity which is allowed and accepted as part of the game.

It is like a soccer game, where every player of the rival team is marked. By keeping a close eye on the moves of the rival players, you can plan your own moves. If you're smart enough and quick enough you'll be victorious.

Seven Stories for Salespeople

IF I DON'T GO, I DON'T GET.

- In the southern part of the United States, an old man with a rowboat ferries passenger across a mile-wide river for ten cents.

- Asked how many times a day he does this, the boatman said, "As many times as I can because the more, I go, the more I get. And, if I don't go, I don't get."

- That's all you need to know-all there is to know-about selling.

ASK YOUR CUSTOMERS…

- An American dog food company held monthly sales promotion meetings, but the chairman was frustrated with the bombastic theories and stale ideas that came forth.

- In the hope of fresh thinking he invited some young trainees to the next meeting, and casually asked one of them what he had to say.

- "Sir, we want to sell dog food and therefore we should ask the dogs what they like," the trainee said. Uproarious laughter erupted, but the chairman said, "Let's give it a try."

- To the astonishment of all, a few dogs were brought in and different varieties of dog food placed before them. The dogs sniffed at all of them. And then zeroed in on two or three.

- The company concentrated its efforts on marketing those few formulations. Within six months, market share registered a 10 percent increase.

JUDGE BY SALES, NOT BY REPORTS.

- A recently employed area salesman in the farm machinery industry wrote his first report to head office. It stunned the sales manager, as it was obvious the new man was almost illiterate:

Dear Bos,

I bin to sea this outfit what an never bawt a pennies-worth of farming mashins form us, an I sole them our know forig arvesters, balin mashins, muk spreaders, an kuters also fifte ov owr knew shift in mashins.

This amounts too a cuppla hundred thowsan pownds ov guds. I am now going to Nawthwn Egerland.

- Before the illiterate could be terminated, another note from him came from Northern Ireland:

Dear Bos,

I cum ere an sole them a half ov a mulyun.

- Not knowing what do do, the sales manager dumped the problem in the chairman's lap. The next morning the salesman's letters were posted on the notice board, along with this memo from the chairman:

We bin spending two much tyme tryeing to spel rite instedd of tryeing to sel. Lett's watch those sails. I want everybodies shud read these letters from owr knew man, who is on the rode do in a grate job for us an you shud goe out an du like he dun.

The difference between you and, me is only of Hearing; where you hear a door close, I hear it open.

WHERE YOU HEAR A DOOR CLOSE, I HEAR IT OPEN...

- A salesman was sent to an island to explore the possibility of selling shoes.

- He did not find a single person wearing shoes on the island, and sent a gloomy report back to the head office that there was no prospect of shoe sales there as no one wore shoes.

- The organisation was reluctant to give up and sent their ace salesman to the same island.

- Within days he was back at head office with a twinkle in his eye: the untapped potential for selling shoes in enormous, he reported.

IDENTIFY YOUR WEAK LINK ...AND ACT NOW!

THE WAR WAS LOST BECAUSE OF A NAIL.

- Centuries ago, a battle was fought which changed the destiny of a state and the people living in it. This state had an excellent army that was well-equipped.

- On the day of the battle, the king was ploughing through the enemy's forces when suddenly his horse tumbled because the shoe on its front foot came off. That was it: the king fell, his forces fled, and the battle was lost.

- When the opposing king analysed the reasons for his unexpected victory, he found that though the king's horse had excellent armour, the nails in his shoes were worn out.

- He learned the lesson: *a chain is only as strong as its weakest link.*

- A large sale may be lost because the pages of the quotation were wrongly stapled and thus did not make any sense.

BE CLEAR ABOUT YOUR MARKET SEGMENT.

- A man went into an insurance office to have his life insured.
- The agent asked, "Do you drive the car a great deal?"
- "No," the man replied.
- "Do you fly much?" the agent continued.
- "No," replied the applicant.
- "Sorry, sir," said the agent. "We no longer insure pedestrians."

A salesman is not a beggar.

SALESMEN ARE NOT ORDER-TAKERS.

- A young lady walked into a store and asked for a hairclip. She selected one and was told it cost Rs. 4. "Your price is too high," she said, and proceeded to haggle.

- After a lot of back and forth the salesman brought down the price to Rs. 2. "Oh, no, not at all," said the lady, and he dropped it to Rs. 1. "You must be joking," said the lady.

- Irritated, the salesman said, "Madam, please spare me-you may take it free." The lady's reply? "Well, in that case, give me two!"

- Everyone is looking for bargains in life. Poor salespeople are too easily intimidated by customers' price objections and give in to get the order.

- These people are not salespeople; they are order-takers. And as is rightly said: anyone can sell a one-dollar article for 99 cents.

Nine Sales Objections and How to Handle Them

'No' and 'yes' are short words that need long thought.

No.

- It is the easiest thing for our boss, the customer, to say. The salesperson who accepts the no at face value is sure to leave his profession in no time.

- "No" does not mean "Never"-therefore, persist.

- There really is no such thing as "No" all by itself. It is always, "No, because…".

- Behind the no you might discover that the prospect:
    + has not applied his mind to evaluate your brand
    + has a friend whose machine of your make isn't working
    + lacks the finance to buy your product
    + does not have the authority to buy
- Try to overcome the problem, but never argue with the prospect and be patient in answering his questions.
- Keep listening for buying signals.

THE COST IS LONG FORGOTTEN BUT THE QUALITY IS REMEMBERED FOREVER.

I CAN'T AFFORD IT.

- This is a strong buying signal. Probably the prospect has evaluated your product and is interested.

- Big numbers put a psychological fear into everyone, the fear of making a wrong decision. The prospect may need more assurance.

- If you've done your research and homework, you'll be prepared to explain the value of the product.

- Make sure the prospect understands the "total cost" involved: the price per se may be high, but the total cost is lower in the long run.

- You may like to develop profit planner formats for your products.

Have you "turned off" the prospect?

I AM NOT INTERESTED.

- Check to make sure you're talking to the individual with authority to buy.

- Probe to find out whether he really means, "I am not interested *at this time...*" If so, organise a follow-up visit.

- Make sure you've adequately researched the prospect, and covered his specific interests.

- Make sure you present the benefits of your product, not just its features.

- Have you turned the prospect off with any of the five no-no's?

+ coming ill-prepared

+ *not using visuals, testimonials, leaflets*

+ *doing a lot of superfluous talking*

+ *being too lazy to demonstrate*

+ *not even asking for the order*

Find out what help he needs to say yes.

I WILL THINK IT OVER.

- The prospect needs help to say yes; try to find out what kind of help.

- Have you presented too many choices, and confused the prospect? It is always better to say convincingly that you feel product C will be ideal for the prospect, based on what he's told you of his needs.

- Encourage the prospect to examine your proposal very carefully. Ask him what other information he needs while thinking it over.

- Help the prospect to draw up a Balance Sheet on the proposal; a list of the pluses and minuses as he sees it. (Make sure the list of pluses is longer!)

- Now is the time to throw in the special inducement you've been holding back. An early-order discount, special payment terms, etc. can push the prospect into talking the decision now.

You're got to find out what the prospect really means.

COME BACK IN THIRTY DAYS.

- Is it a brush-off, a stall, or a sincere statement? Try to find out, and proceed accordingly.

- If it's a stall for legitimate concerns or a sincere statement, you can give several options, such as:

+ *Well, we can deliver now and you can pay us in 30 days...*

+ *Would you like me to meet someone else in your organisation? ...*

+ *Right now, we have a sales-incentive scheme going on and you can take advantage of it...*

- Do not leave empty-handed; get some sort of commitment:

+ *that he will buy after 30 days*

+ *that he will meet you in 30 days*

+ *that he will suggest some more prospects*

- Set up the next appointment.

Don't "paper" the prospect.

JUST LEAVE ME YOUR LITERATURE.

- Never just leave your leaflet. Find out the why of the prospect's response. Is it lack of interest? Lack of time? Another pressing problem? Should you meet someone else?

- Once you decide to leave literature, mark it up for the prospect's convenience in focussing on his needs.

- Write a thank-you note mentioning specific points.

- Try not to leave the literature without a three-minute drill, with specific motivation for the prospect to go over the literature.

- Do not "paper" the prospect, dumping piles of literature on him aimlessly.

Nothing is ever permanent.

I AM HAPPY WITH MY PRESENT DEALER.

- Nothing is ever perfect or permanent. Sometimes the best marriages end up in divorce. Nothing is certain in life except change.

- The present dealer may develop problems: quality-control problems, financial crises, partnership problems. His salesman may neglect the account, or be transferred and replaced by someone the prospect dislikes.

- The good salesperson is so persistent that when the prospect needs a change, he will be the only person in the prospect's mind.

Don't get rattled… Everyone is different.

MY JOB IS DIFFERENT.

- You have to agree! Everybody is different. There are more than 5 billion human beings on this earth and no two are alike.

- But don't leave it at that. Ask him to educate you on how his business is different, and then sell to that difference.

- Find out what he likes about his situation, what he is proud of and wouldn't change, what he is dissatisfied with and wants to improve, and what his long-range goals and dreams are.

- Use the prospect's conviction of his uniqueness to position your product or service as the only which can fit the situation.

"Can I let you know tomorrow? It takes me a while to reach a consensus."

I'LL HAVE TO TALK IT OVER WITH MY FATHER.

- Any major purchase involves more than one person. It could be a father, uncles, friends, colleagues, or a committee...

- Keep asking, keep digging. Learn more about everybody who might be involved in the decision.

- With the prospect's help, meet the influencers.

- Research what the influencer is looking for in your product.

- Use visuals and dramatize your points in group presentations. Address the concerns of all present.

HUMAN PROGRESS IS NEITHER AUTOMATIC NOR INEVITABLE...THIS IS NO TIME FOR APATHY OR COMPLACENCY. THIS IS A TIME FOR VIGOROUS AND POSITIVE ACTION.

-Martin Luther King

I WILL WAIT UNTIL BUSINESS IS BETTER.

- If it's not a brush-off, this objection simply tells you that the question, "Why buy now?" has not been answered to the prospect's satisfaction.

- Keep a few incentives in your pocket for this moment, to goad the prospect into action now. Things like a special price that will be raised soon, special payment terms, free delivery/installation, extended warranty, etc.

- Review the benefits to be derived by accepting your proposal.

- Light a spark of enthusiasm. Remember: business never gets better tomorrow; it has to be made better with better ways, sound risk-taking and positive thinking.

Water the plant of fortune with drops of sweat. And see it grow and bear fruit!

The Secret of Selling Well

THE RATIO BETWEEN HARDWORK AND LUCK IS 70:30.

Make hard work a daily habit.

Selling well is doing certain things...a certain way...every day...

The water of the Bhakra Dam turns into light and power only when it is harnesses. No horse gets anywhere until it is harnessed. And no life ever grows unless it is focussed, dedicated and disciplined.

- A professional salesperson must work, physically and mentally, according to his action plan, and the plan must be prepared on a daily, weekly, monthly, quarterly and yearly basis.

- *A professional salesperson* must be faithful to himself, to his company and to his prospect. Honesty is the best policy, even when it seems you can't afford it.

- *A professional salesperson* will do his best to learn everything about his work and his company and his prospect, and will continue to grow as a person.

- *A professional salesperson* will keep the company of those who have an obsession for doing their jobs well. Selling is applied common sense, but it takes a good deal of training to sharpen the common sense.

- *A professional salesperson* makes sure he always has a positive attitude. The two main ingredients are enthusiasm and confidence. Enthusiasm comes from within, but it is based on knowing your product very well and understanding how it can benefit your customers.

- *A professional salesperson* makes sure he knows his selling techniques well, and how and when to use them. This breeds confidence. He never forgets that the customer has to shell out hard-earned money for his product.

- *A professional salesperson* knows how to analyse successes and failures, and build on them. This is another confidence-spinner.

Remember!

Success is a Journey, Not a Destination!

***

www.ingramcontent.com/pod-product-compliance
Lightning Source LLC
Chambersburg PA
CBHW072016230526
45468CB00021B/1614